T0195599

BOOK 2

GRADES 4–5

# MATH
## EXTENSION UNITS

Written by Judy Leimbach and Kathy Leimbach
Illustrated by Mary Lou Johnson

**Geometry • Fractions • Graphing • Problem Solving**

First published in 2007 by Prufrock Press Inc.

Published in 2021 by Routledge
605 Third Avenue, New York, NY 10017
2 Park Square, Milton Park, Abingdon, Oxon OX14 4RN

*Routledge is an imprint of the Taylor & Francis Group, an informa business*

Copyright © 2007 Taylor & Francis Group

ISBN: 9781593631000 (pbk)

DOI: 10.4324/9781003236481

# Table of Contents

# Math Extension Units, Book 2

| Unit | Common Core State Standards in Math |
|---|---|
| Computation and Problem Solving | 4.OA.A Use the four operations with whole numbers to solve problems.<br>4.NBT.B Use place value understanding and properties of operations to perform multi-digit arithmetic.<br>4.MD.A Solve problems involving measurement and conversion of measurements.<br>5.NBT.B Perform operations with multi-digit whole numbers and with decimals to hundredths.<br>6.RP.A Understand ratio concepts and use ratio reasoning to solve problems.<br>6.G.A Solve real-world and mathematical problems involving area, surface area, and volume. |
| Angles, Triangles, and Other Polygons | 4.G.A Draw and identify lines and angles, and classify shapes by properties of their lines and angles.<br>7.G.A Draw construct, and describe geometrical figures and describe the relationships between them.<br>7.G.B Solve real-life and mathematical problems involving angle measure, area, surface area, and volume.<br>8.G.A Understand congruence and similarity using physical models, transparencies, or geometry software. |
| Fractions | 4.NF.A Extend understanding of fraction equivalence and ordering.<br>4.NF.B Build fractions from unit fractions.<br>4.MD.A Solve problems involving measurement and conversion of measurements.<br>5.NF.A Use equivalent fractions as a strategy to add and subtract fractions.<br>5.NF.B Apply and extend previous understandings of multiplication and division.<br>6.RP.A Understand ratio concepts and use ratio reasoning to solve problems. |
| Graphs | 4.NF.A Extend understanding of fraction equivalence and ordering.<br>4.NF.C Understand decimal notation for fractions, and compare decimal fractions.<br>5.NF.B Apply and extend previous understandings of multiplication and division.<br>5.G.A Graph points on the coordinate plane to solve real-world and mathematical problems.<br>6.RP.A Understand ratio concepts and use ratio reasoning to solve problems. |

Key:
OA = Operations & Algebraic Thinking; NBT = Number & Operations in Base Ten; NF = Number & Operations--Fractions; MD = Measurement & Data; G = Geometry; RP = Ratios & Proportional Relationships

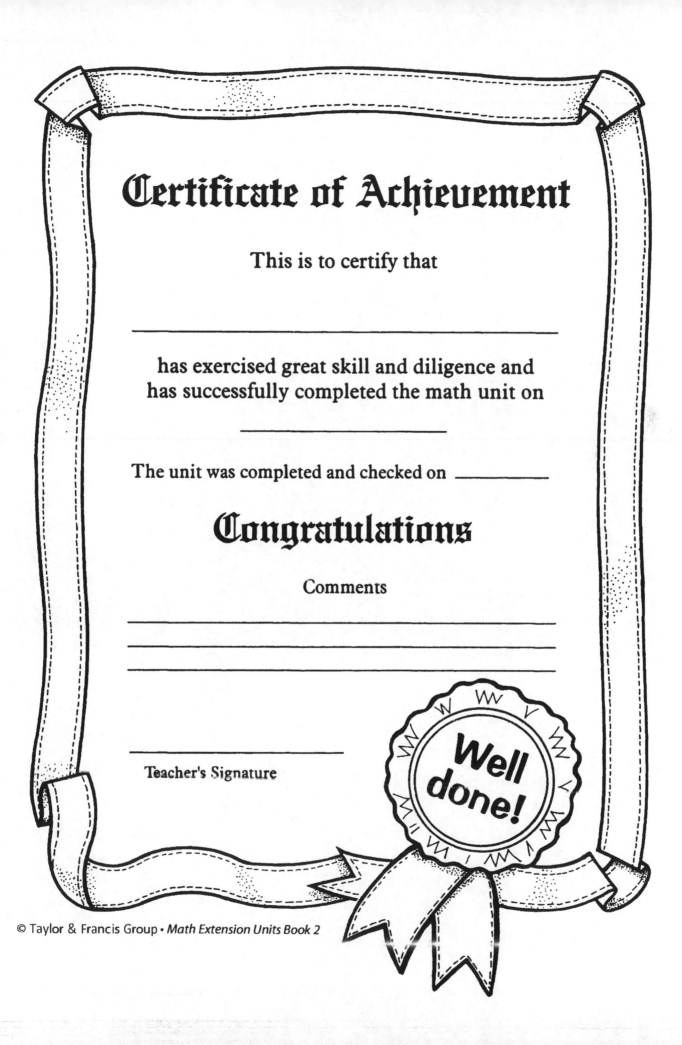

# Certificate of Achievement

This is to certify that

_____

has exercised great skill and diligence and
has successfully completed the math unit on

_____

The unit was completed and checked on _____

# Congratulations

Comments

_____
_____
_____

_____
Teacher's Signature

Well
done!

# Information for the Instructor

The purpose of this book is to help busy classroom teachers provide for those students who quickly grasp the mathematical concepts being taught and are ready to move on to more challenging material. The extension activities provided in the four units of this book will help students expand their knowledge in each area and give them opportunities to apply their skills in a variety of different ways. The units include challenging activities that will require higher-level thinking and will broaden students' problem solving skills.

Our most able students should be encouraged to stretch their thinking, to expand their learning, and to develop perseverance. It is the teacher's responsibility to provide them with opportunities to do so and to encourage them in their efforts. These units provide a way for teachers to easily offer these kinds of educational experiences for their able math students.

## How to Use the Units

The materials in this book may be used for the whole class or as extension units for individuals or small groups. The units were designed primarily to meet the needs of students who learn quickly, work at a fast pace, and are capable of going beyond the regular mathematics curriculum at their grade level.

The units in this book correspond to topics usually included in the intermediate mathematics curriculum. Each unit provides meaningful extension activities that advanced math students could work on while their classmates are mastering the more basic concepts. The pages in each section can be compiled into a packet with the assignment sheet as the cover page and given to each student to work on independently. The units also can also be arranged in a math center with each student having an individual folder, using the assignment sheet to record progress.

## Problem Solving

This unit includes problems requiring all four basic operations. The problems are based on real-life situations. This unit does not need to be done in the order presented; however, the latter pages require knowledge of calculating averages, area, and perimeter. Students will need to choose a strategy for solving the problems in this unit, and may need to use more than one set of computations to arrive at some of the answers. You may choose to allow students to use a calculator for the computations on some of the pages or to check their work when completed.

## Angles, Triangles, and Other Polygons

Before beginning this unit, students should know how to use a protractor to measure and draw angles. The unit is sequential, progressing through measuring and drawing angles, drawing and measuring different types of triangles, finding angle measurements from given information instead of using a protractor, to constructing symmetrical geometric designs with regular polygons.

## Fractions

Before beginning this unit, students should have a basic understanding of fractions. The activities in this unit are sequential, with the first four pages covering comparing, ordering, reducing, adding, and subtracting fractions and mixed numbers. The next ten pages present real-life situations requiring these skills.

## Graphs

This unit covers a variety of types of graphs, including picture graphs, double bar graphs, multiple line graphs, and circle graphs. The activities require students to interpret data from each type of graph and to construct graphs of their own from given data. Students need to know how to use a protractor and how to multiply fractions for the two pages requiring them to draw circle graphs. The last two pages have the students locate graphs to interpret and gather data for an original graph.

# Assignment Sheet
## Computation and Problem Solving

Name _____

I began this unit on _____ (date)

Mark off each activity after you have completed it and after it has been checked. Hand in all pages when you finish the unit.

| Lesson | Completed | Checked |
|---|---|---|
| 1. Feeding the Animals | _____ | _____ |
| 2. Planning a Trip | _____ | _____ |
| 3. Patriotic Puzzles | _____ | _____ |
| 4. Planning a Picnic | _____ | _____ |
| 5. Summer Job | _____ | _____ |
| 6. Field Trip | _____ | _____ |
| 7. All Aboard! | _____ | _____ |
| 8. Class Store | _____ | _____ |
| 9. The Basketball Game | _____ | _____ |
| 10. Buying Tile | _____ | _____ |
| 11. Buying Carpeting | _____ | _____ |
| 12. Redecorating | _____ | _____ |

I completed this unit on _____ (date)

# Feeding the Animals

Name_____

It takes a lot of money to feed all the animals in a big city zoo. At the Brookfield Zoo in Brookfield, Illinois, a variety of foods is needed to meet the nutritional requirements of more than 2,000 animals.

1.  Fruits and vegetables are the major dietary ingredient for many of the small mammals, birds, and primates. The zoo's yearly consumption of fresh fruits and vegetables is about 312,000 pounds a year, at a cost of about $97,500.

    How many pounds of fruits and vegetables would it take to feed the animals for one month? _____

    How much would one month's supply cost?         _____

2.  The zoo purchases over 25 different types of grains at a yearly cost of $80,000. The biggest eaters of grains are the hoofed animals. The hoofed animals and the pachyderms also consume over 20,000 bales of hay each year. The total hay costs are about $64,000 per year.

    What is the cost of the grain and hay for one year? _____

    For one month? _____

3.  Over 100,000 pounds of fish are given to the animals each year. The bears consume over 3,650 pounds, but the majority of the fish (about 82,000 pounds) is consumed by the dolphins and other animals at the "Seven Seas" exhibit. It costs about $60,000 a year to provide this fish for the animals.

    How many pounds of fish a day do the bears eat? _____

    How much per month does the zoo spend on fish? _____

4.  Each year the carnivores and omnivores at the zoo eat about 108,000 pounds of meat. The omnivores eat a fourth of the meat products.

    How many pounds of meat do the carnivores eat in a year? _____

# Planning a Trip

Name _____

Matt's older brother promised to take him and
two of his friends on a trip to Washington, D.C.,
if each of the boys could raise the money for the
trip. They agreed to split all the costs equally
between the four of them. Using the figures below,
find how much money each boy would need.

- ◆ Round trip plane tickets were $162 each.
- ◆ Renting a car for four days would cost $29 per day.
- ◆ The hotel rooms were $84 per night. (They need 2 rooms for 3 nights.)
- ◆ They ordered tickets for a baseball game that cost $15 each.
- ◆ They estimated food would cost them each $25 a day.
- ◆ They figured each person should take $100 for other expenses.

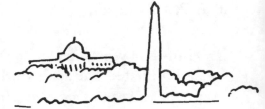

1.  The total cost of the trip per person would be $_____


Matt already has $140 in the bank but he has to raise the rest of the money he needs for his trip.

- ◆ He mowed lawns for $10 for a small lawn and $15 for a large lawn. In three weeks he was
  able to cut 8 small lawns and 6 large lawns. He had to spend $20 on garbage bags.
- ◆ He baby-sat 2 hours a day for 8 days. For this he earned $5.00 an hour. He spent $4.00 on ice
  cream and candy for the kids.
- ◆ For his birthday, Matt's Aunt Kathy gave him $50 for his trip.
- ◆ He earned $20 watering the Smiths' plants while they were on vacation.
- ◆ He washed four cars and charged $10 for each car.
- ◆ He earned another $30 cleaning out the garage for his parents.

2.  At this point does Matt have enough money for the trip?

No - He still needed to raise $ _____ more .

Yes - He has exactly the right amount.

Yes - He has $ _____ more than he needed.

# Patriotic Puzzles

Name_____

While visiting Washington, D.C., Matt's older brother made up some interesting puzzles for him to figure out.

1. Each column in the Lincoln Memorial represents a state in the Union at the time of Lincoln's death. When the memorial was dedicated in 1922, there were 12 more states in the Union. Since that time, two more states have joined the Union.

   How many columns are there in the Lincoln Memorial? _____

2. The dome of the Capitol building is 275 feet shorter than the Washington Monument. The total height of the two buildings is 835 feet.

   How tall is the Washington Monument? _____

3. The John F. Kennedy Center for Performing Arts houses 6 theaters. The total seating capacity for all six theaters is 6,950 seats. The largest theater seats 150 more than the second largest theater. The four small theaters all together seat 750.

   How many seats are in the largest theater? _____

4. Thomas Jefferson was 33 years old when he wrote the Declaration of Independence in 1776. He and John Adams, our second president, both died on the 4th of July exactly 50 years after the signing of the Declaration of Independence. Their combined ages when they died were 173 years.

   How old was John Adams when he died? _____

5. One day Matt and his brother planned on visiting four different memorials — the Lincoln Memorial, Vietnam Veterans Memorial, the Washington Monument, and the Jefferson Memorial.

   How many different routes are possible to visit all four memorials? _____

# Planning a Picnic

Name _____

The neighbors on Willow Road have a neighborhood picnic every summer. This year they have planned for 100 people to attend.

1. The picnic committee members made a list of everything they would need. Complete the shopping list below by filling in the number of packages of each item they will need to buy to have enough for 100 people. Then show how many of each item will be left over.

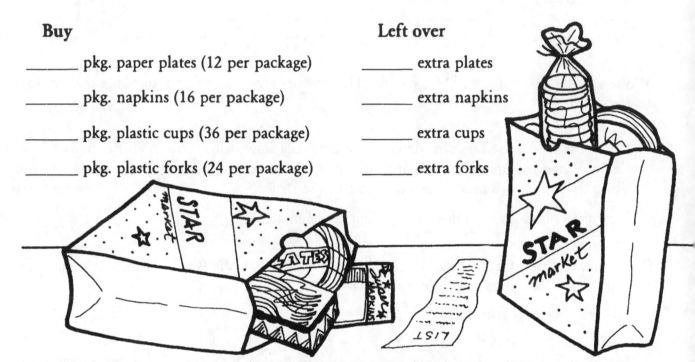

**Buy**

_____ pkg. paper plates (12 per package)

_____ pkg. napkins (16 per package)

_____ pkg. plastic cups (36 per package)

_____ pkg. plastic forks (24 per package)

**Left over**

_____ extra plates

_____ extra napkins

_____ extra cups

_____ extra forks

2. Hot dogs and buns come 8 to a package. Soda comes 24 cans to a case or 6 cans to a carton. The committee members decided they could serve 14 people with a large bag of chips. The cookies they are buying come in packages of 3 dozen cookies each. They figure they can serve 12 people with each half gallon of ice cream. They want to buy enough for each person at the picnic to have 3 cookies. Complete the shopping list below by filling in the number of packages of each item they will need.

_____ pkg. hot dogs

_____ pkg. buns

_____ cases and _____ cartons of soda

_____ large bags of chips

_____ pkg. cookies

_____ half gallons of ice cream

# Summer Job

Name_____

Jenny has a summer job as a lifeguard at the city pool. Do the following problems to get information about her job.

1. Jenny works from 11:00 a.m. until 6:30 p.m. five days a week. She get a half an hour for lunch, for which she does not get paid.

   If she earns $6.00 an hour, how much does she earn in a week (5 days)? _____

2. The lifeguards get paid every two weeks. Taxes and Social Security are taken out of their checks. Jenny's first check was for $323.30.

   How much was taken out of her check for taxes and Social Security? _____

3. When Jenny cashed her check, she kept out $50 and put the rest in the bank. She put twice as much in her savings account as in her checking account.

   How much did she put in each account? _____ savings _____ checking

4. Jenny will work at the pool for 10 weeks during the summer. At the end of her sixth week she will get a 50 cent an hour raise. She works the same hours every day, five days a week.

   What will her total earnings (before taxes and Social Security) be for the entire summer?

   _____

5. Jenny's brother makes money during the summer mowing lawns. He cuts three lawns a day and charges $11 per lawn. He works six days a week and does not pay any taxes.

   Who will make the most money during the summer? _____

   Explain your answer. _____

# Field Trip

Name _____

The four fifth-grade classes from Lincoln School went on a field trip to the art museum. The classes together had 112 students and 4 teachers. Here are some facts about the trip.

- The teachers divided the students into groups of 8 and took one parent along to supervise each group of students.
- They went in buses that each had seats for 66 people. It cost $136.50 to rent a bus.
- The cost to enter the museum was $2.00 for students and $3.50 for adults.
- Each student took a sack lunch, but they bought drinks in the lunchroom at the museum for 75¢ each.
- In the lunchroom, the students did not all sit with their groups because each of the tables seated 12 people.

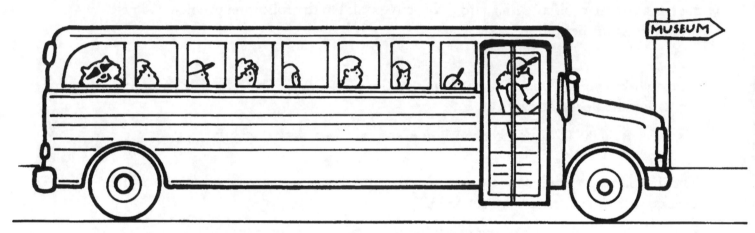

1. How many parents did they need to take along on the trip? _____

2. How many people went on the trip altogether? _____

3. How much did they have to pay to rent buses? _____

   How many extra seats did they have left on the buses? _____

4. What was the total cost for the whole group to enter the museum? _____

5. How many tables did the whole group need for lunch? _____

6. What was the total cost of the field trip ?_____

   (Include the price of the buses, entrance to the museum for everyone, and drinks only for the students.)

7. If everyone (adults and children) is charged $4.00, will that cover the cost of the trip? _____

# All Aboard!

Name_____

1. Commuter trains leave every 20 minutes from 6:00 a.m. through 9:00 a.m. and every 30 minutes until 9:00 p.m.

   How many trains leave the station from 6:00 a.m. through 4:00 p.m.? _____ trains

2. Mr. and Mrs. Jordan spend $620 for tickets for themselves and their children. They have four children. The fares from Brownstone to Salem are:
   - $140 - adult 18 and over
   - $90 - children ages 6-17
   - $70 - children under 6 years

   How many of the children are under 6 years old? _____

3. A train that runs from Union Station to Center City passes through Yorkville and Alton on the way. The distance from Union Station to Yorkville is half the distance from Yorkville to Alton. The distance from Alton to Center City is three times the distance from Union Station to Yorkville. It is 114 miles from Alton to Center City.

   How far is it from Union Station to Center City?

   _____ miles

4. The fare on a commuter train from Belleville to Metropolis is $1.20 for adults and 75¢ for children. The conductor collects $19.80 from the people who got on in Belleville and plan to get off in Metropolis. There are ten more adults on the train as there are children.

   How many children's fares are paid?

   _____ children's fares

# Class Store

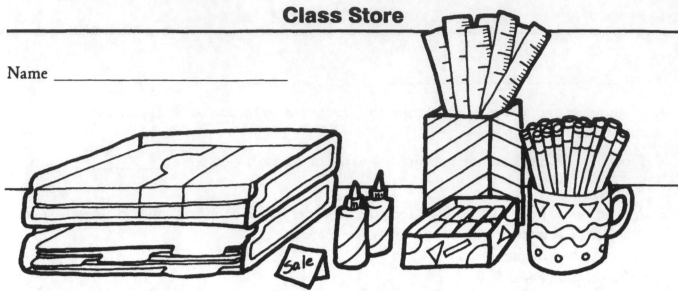

Name _____

The sixth grade classes were raising money for an end-of-the-year trip to the state capital. To raise the $400 they needed for the trip they set up a class store to sell school supplies to students before school and during lunch hours. The chart below shows how much they paid for the supplies they sold and how much they charged for each item. Use the facts in the chart to figure out how much profit they made on each item.

| Item | Amount Paid | Price Charged |
|------|-------------|---------------|
| Pencils | $4.76 per gross | 12¢ each |
| Erasers | $9.00 per hundred | 25¢ each |
| Paper | 39¢ a pack | 75¢ a pack |
| Rulers | $1.56 a dozen | 30¢ each |
| Glue | $5.00 per box of 20 bottles | 65¢ a bottle |
| Folders | $12.00 per hundred | 30¢ each |

1. They bought 250 packs of paper and sold every one. Their profit was $ _____.

2. They bought 3 boxes of pencils that each contained a gross (144). They sold 415 pencils. Their profit was $ _____.

3. They bought 9 dozen rulers and sold all but 3 of them. Their profit was $ _____

4. They bought 100 bottles of glue and sold 89 of them. Their profit was $ _____

5. They bought 200 folders and sold them all. Their profit was $ _____

6. They bought 200 erasers and sold 182 of them. Their profit was $ _____

7. Their total profit from the store was $ _____

8. How much money did they need to raise from other projects to fund their trip? $ _____

# The Basketball Game

Name_____

When the Wildcats played the Huskies, the Wildcats won by a score of 88 to 82. The charts below show the records for the five starting players on each team.

## Wildcats

| Player | Baskets (2 pts.) | 3-pt. Shots | Free Throws (1 pt.) | Total Pts. |
|---|---|---|---|---|
| R. Henley | 3 | 1 | 2 | |
| J. Rodriguez | 4 | 0 | 4 | |
| B. Cassidy | 6 | 2 | 4 | |
| M. Johnson | 4 | 1 | 1 | |
| F. Yung | 7 | 1 | 1 | |
| Team Totals | | | | |

## Huskies

| Player | Baskets (2 pts.) | 3-pt. Shots | Free Throws (1 pt.) | Total Pts. |
|---|---|---|---|---|
| B. Hunt | 3 | 0 | 2 | |
| M. Williams | 4 | 0 | 2 | |
| W. Delaney | 5 | 2 | 4 | |
| M. Gonzales | 8 | 0 | 3 | |
| S. Kaminski | 4 | 1 | 2 | |
| Team Totals | | | | |

Fill in the boxes in the charts above with the total number points for each starting player and the team totals. Then answer the questions below.

1. How many points did the other players on each team score?

   Wildcats _____     Huskies _____

2. Who was the highest scorer on each team?

   Wildcats _____     Huskies _____

3. What was the average score for the starting players on each team?

   Wildcats _____     Huskies _____

# Buying Tile

Name _____

The Sanchez family is putting in new tile floors in the kitchen and two bathrooms of their house. Use the dimensions and price per square foot for tiles to figure the area of each room and the cost for tile.

| Room | Dimensions | Price/sq. ft. | Area | Tile Cost |
|---|---|---|---|---|
| kitchen | 16' x 12' | $2.75 | | |
| children's bath | 6' x 8' | $2.25 | | |
| parents' bath | 8' x 10' | $2.50 | | |

1. It will cost the Sanchez family a total of $_____ to put new tile in their home.

2. How much will they save if they put the same tile in the parents' bathroom as they chose for the children's bathroom? _____

3. What are the dimensions of the bathroom in your home? _____ by _____

   What is the area? _____

4. How much would it cost to tile the floor in your bath with the same tile the Sanchez family selected for the children's bath? _____

# Buying Carpeting

Name_____

The Kuharik family is choosing the carpeting for the family room, dining room, and bedrooms in their new house. They can spend up to $2400. The carpeting they chose for the family room and the dining room costs $25 per square yard. The carpeting for the parent's bedroom costs $22 per square yard, and for the two children's bedrooms the carpet costs $16 per square yard.

Figure the cost of the flooring for each room by calculating the area of each room, the number of square yards of carpeting that will be needed, and the cost of the carpeting.

| Room | Dimension | Area (sq. ft.) | Area (sq. yds.) | Cost |
|---|---|---|---|---|
| family room | 16' x 18' | | | |
| dining room | 12' x 12' | | | |
| parents' bedroom | 14' x 18' | | | |
| Leah's bedroom | 9' x 14' | | | |
| John's bedroom | 9' x 12' | | | |

How much will it cost to carpet all five rooms?   $ _____

**Note:**

*Carpeting is sold in square yards. To figure out how much carpeting is needed, convert the area from square feet to square yards by dividing by 9, because there are 9 square feet in a square yard. For example, if the area of a room is 117 square foot you would divide 117 by 9 to get 13 square yards.*

# Redecorating

Name _____

Shelly is planning to redecorate her room. She is going to paint the walls and then put a 6-inch wallpaper border around the top of the room. She is also planning to carpet the floor.

1. Shelly has two walls that are 8 feet high and 18 feet long and two other two walls that are 8 feet high and 14 feet long.

   What is the surface area of the four walls of her room? _____

2. If one gallon of paint covers 350 square feet, how many gallons of paint will she need to buy to put two coats of paint on her walls? The paint she is buying is sold in gallon cans only.

   _____ gallons

3. To purchase carpet, she must first find the area of the floor and then convert the area in square feet to square yards, since carpeting is sold in yards, not feet.

   What is the area of the floor? _____ square feet or

   _____ square yards.

4. How many feet of wallpaper border will she need to go around the room? _____ feet

5. Using the prices in the chart, figure how much it will cost Shelly to redecorate her room.

| Item | Price | Amount Needed | Cost |
|---|---|---|---|
| paint | $8.99 per gallon | | |
| carpet | $18.95 / sq. yd. | | |
| wallpaper border | $7.95 per 5-yard roll | | |

It will cost $_____ for Shelly to redecorate her room.

# Assignment Sheet

## Angles, Triangles and Other Polygons

Name_____

I began this unit on _____ (date)

Mark off each activity after you have completed it and after it has been checked.
Hand in all pages when you finish the unit.

| Lesson | Completed | Checked |
|---|---|---|
| **1.** Drawing Angles | _____ | _____ |
| **2.** Drawing Pairs of Angles | _____ | _____ |
| **3.** Types of Triangles | _____ | _____ |
| **4.** Triangle Experiment | _____ | _____ |
| **5.** Naming Triangles | _____ | _____ |
| **6.** Missing Angles | _____ | _____ |
| **7.** Regular Polygons and Angles | _____ | _____ |
| **8.** Lines of Symmetry | _____ | _____ |
| **9.** Symmetry Experiment | _____ | _____ |
| **10.** Rotation Symmetry and Design | _____ | _____ |
| **11.** Hexagon Design | _____ | _____ |
| **12.** Decagon Design | _____ | _____ |

I completed this unit on _____ (date)

right triangle   acute triangle

# Vocabulary

| | | |
|---|---|---|
| **Line** | | A set of points that extends in both directions infinitely. |
| **Ray** | | A straight line extending from a point. |
| **Line Segment** | | Part of a straight line. |
| **Angle** | | A geometric figure formed by two rays with a common point (vertex). |
| **Acute angle** | | An angle between 0° and 90°. |
| **Right angle** | | An angle that is 90°. |
| **Obtuse angle** | | An angle between 90° and 180°. |
| **Straight angle** | | An angle that measures 180° and forms a straight line. |
| **Polygon** | | A closed figure made of line segments. If it has equal angles and sides, it is a regular polygon. |
| **Adjacent angles** | | Two angles with a common side and a common vertex. |
| **Linear Pair** | | Two adjacent angles whose non-common sides form a straight line. |
| **Vertical angles** | | Two angles formed by two intersecting lines that are not adjacent angles. Vertical angles have equal measures. |

20

# Drawing Angles

Angle ABC can be written as ∠ABC, which denotes an angle with a point A on one ray, a point C on the other ray, and point B as the vertex . To show the measure of this angle you can write "m ∠ABC = 30º," which means "the measure of angle ABC is 30º."

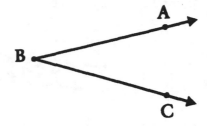

Draw and label the following angles.

1. Draw ∠XYZ so that m∠XYZ is 12º more that m∠ABC.

2. Draw ∠TQR so that m∠TQR is three times m∠ABC.

3. Draw ∠JKL so that m∠JKL is four times m∠XYZ.

4. Draw ∠FDG so that m∠JKL is 35º more than m∠FDG.

# Drawing Pairs of Angles

Name _____

Draw each of the following angles.

| 1. Adjacent angles of 32° and 44° | 2. A linear pair with a 115° angle |
|---|---|
| | |

| 3. A linear pair with equal angles | 4. Vertical angles of 65° |
|---|---|
| | |

# Types of Triangles

Name_____

There are two ways to name triangles — by their **angles** and by their **sides**.

## Names Using Angles

An **acute triangle** has 3 acute angles.
An **obtuse triangle** has 1 obtuse angle.
A **right triangle** has 1 right angle.

## Names Using Sides

An **equilateral triangle** has all sides equal.
A **scalene triangle** has no equal sides.
An **isosceles triangle** has 2 equal sides.

Draw these triangles.

| acute triangle | obtuse triangle | right triangle |
|---|---|---|
| | | |

| equilateral triangle | scalene triangle | isosceles triangle |
|---|---|---|
| | | |

# Triangle Experiment

Name_____

In this experiment you will be tearing off the three angles of a triangle and placing them next to each other to form a straight line.

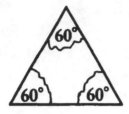

Trace these three types of triangles on another piece of paper. Cut them out, tear off the angles, and place the angles together along a straight line.

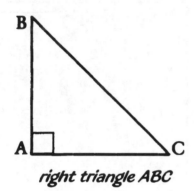

*right triangle ABC*

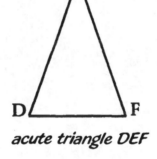

*acute triangle DEF*

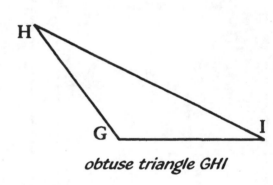

*obtuse triangle GHI*

1. In which of the triangles do the three angles form a straight line when placed next to each other? _____

2. This experiment demonstrates that the sum of the angles of a triangle equals _____°.

3. Find the missing angle in a triangle that has the following two angles.

   a. 90°, 62°, _____°       b. 51°, 39°, _____°       c. 45°, 122°, _____°

4. An equilateral triangle has three equal sides and angles.

   What are the measures of each of the angles? _____

5. Is it possible to have a triangle with two obtuse angles? Explain your answer. _____

   _____

# Naming Triangles

Name _____

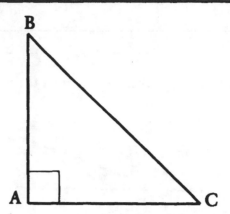

Often triangles are classified by a combination of sides and angles. For example, triangle ABC is a **right isosceles triangle,** because it has one right angle and two equal sides.

1. Combining the triangle names that indicate angles (acute, obtuse, and right) and the triangle names based on the triangle's sides (equilateral, scalene, and isosceles), you have nine possible triangles. Write all the different ways triangles can be named using a combination of names based on angles and names based on sides.

   *acute isosceles*_____     *acute equilateral*_____     _____

   _____     _____     _____

   *right isosceles*_____     _____     _____

2. Circle any triangles in the list that are **not possible** to draw.

3. Draw and label three of the different kinds of triangles.

# Missing Angles

Name _____

Without using a protractor, find the missing angle measurements in these figures.

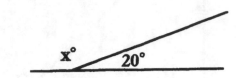

1.   x = _____ °

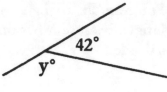

2.   y = _____ °

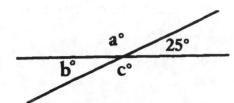

3.   a = _____ °

   b = _____ °

   c = _____ °

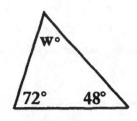

4.   w = _____ °

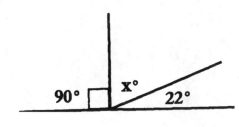

5.   x = _____ °

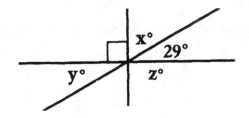

6.   x = _____ °

   y = _____ °

   z = _____ °

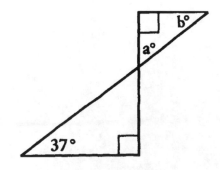

7.   a = _____ °

   b = _____ °

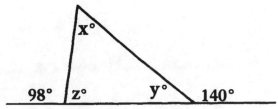

8.   x = _____ °

   y = _____ °

   z = _____ °

# Regular Polygons and Angles

Name_____

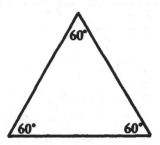

You have already discovered that since the sum of the angles in a triangle is 180° and each that of the angles in an equilateral triangle is 60°.

One way to find the angles in other regular polygons is to divide the polygon into isosceles triangles arranged around a midpoint. The sum of the central angles will always be 360°. Knowing that the sum of the angles in the isosceles triangle is 180°, you can find the measure of the other angles of the triangle and the measure of the angles of the polygon.

Study the first example and then fill in the chart for the other regular polygons.

| Regular Polygon | | Number of Triangles | Central Angle of Triangle | Angle of the Polygon | Sum of Angles in the Polygon |
|---|---|---|---|---|---|
| Square | | 4 | 90° <br><br> ( 360° ÷ 4 = 90°) | 90° <br><br> (45° + 45°=90°) | 360° |
| Pentagon | | | | | |
| Hexagon | | | | | |
| Octagon | | | | | |
| Decagon | | | | | |

# Lines of Symmetry

Name _____

Regular polygons have equal sides and equal
angles. All regular polygons have at least one line
of symmetry (a line that divides the figure so that
the area on one side of the line is an exact
reflection of the area on the other side of the line).

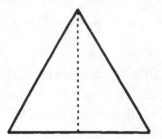

1. One line of symmetry has been drawn for the equilateral triangle above. Draw the other lines
of symmetry.

2. How many lines of symmetry does an equilateral triangle have? _____

3. Draw the lines of symmetry for each of these regular polygons.

**a.** square

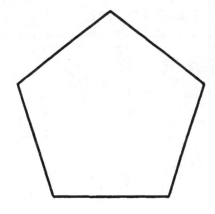

**b.** pentagon

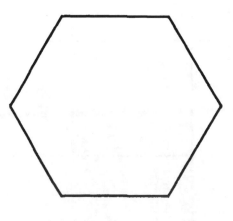

**c.** hexagon

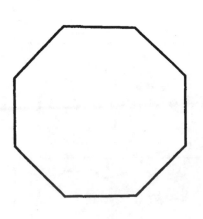

**d.** octagon

# Symmetry Experiment

Name_____

The two triangles on the right are congruent scalene triangles. Cut out one of the triangles and place it on top of the other triangle so that the shapes coincide (point A coincides with point D, point B coincides with point E, and point C coincides with point F). Turn the cut-out triangle in one direction until the shapes coincide again.

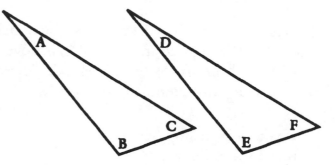

1. Did the triangle you rotated make a complete 360° rotation before the figures matched up again? _____

Repeat the same procedure with the congruent equilateral triangles on the right.

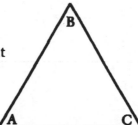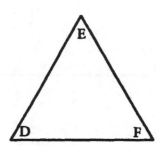

2. Did you make a complete 360° rotation before the figures matched up again? _____

3. How many times did the two triangles coincide in a complete 360° rotation? _____

---

A geometric figure has rotational symmetry if it coincides with its image in less than one full 360° rotation.

---

4. Circle the polygons that have rotational symmetry.

a.          b.          c.

d. 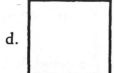         e.          f.

# Rotational Symmetry and Design

Name _____

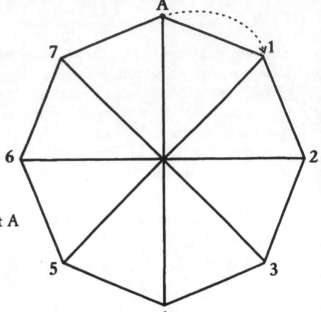

The regular octagon on the right has rotational symmetry. If you place an identical figure over the top of it and turn it 45° to the right, the figures will coincide, with point A in position 1.

1. If you turn the top figure another 45°, where will point A be? _____

2. How many 45° turns will be necessary before point A is back where it started? _____

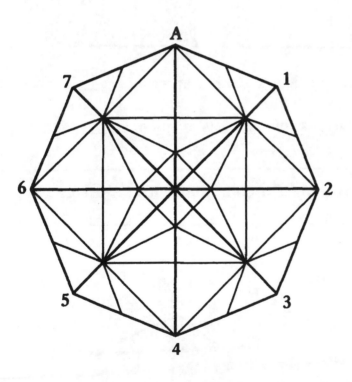

The regular octagon on the left has a **design** with rotational symmetry.

3. If you put an identical figure over this figure and turn it 45° to the right, will the **designs** coincide? _____

4. If you turn the figure another 45° to the right, will the **designs** coincide? _____

5. How many times in a complete 360° rotation will the **designs** coincide? _____

6. Use at least 6 different colors to color the figure so that the colors on the design coincide with each 90° turn.

7. On another piece of paper make a regular polygon with a design in it so that the design has rotational symmetry.

# Hexagon Design

Name_____

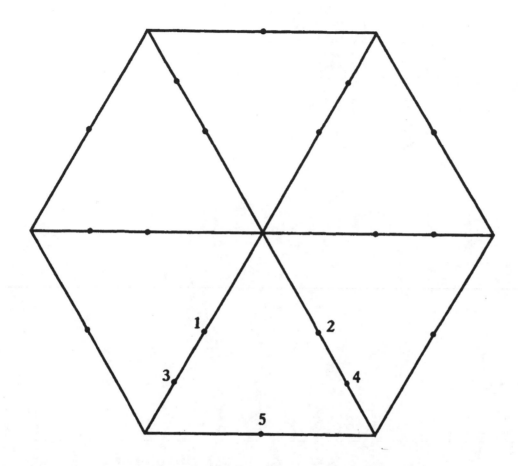

1. Using a straightedge, connect the following points in the hexagon above.

   points 1 and 2         points 2 and 3
   points 3 and 4         points 3 and 5
   points 1 and 4         points 4 and 5

2. To complete a design with rotational symmetry, continue connecting points in the other sections of the hexagon in the same way as in the first section

3. You may add additional points and lines to make a more interesting design. Make sure that your design has rotational symmetry.

4. Use a variety of colors to color your design. Remember to maintain rotational symmetry.

## ON YOUR OWN

**Make your own hexagon design with rotational symmetry.**

Name _____

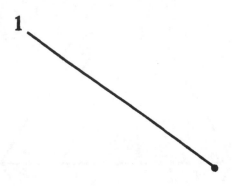

1. Use a protractor to draw a regular decagon by drawing 10 isosceles triangles (with a central angle of 36°) around the midpoint. Make the equal sides of the triangle 6 centimeters long. The first side is drawn for you.

2. Number the first spoke of the design 1. Continue numbering the spokes clockwise around the figure.

3. Mark a point 25 millimeters from the center point on each of the even-numbered spokes.

4. Use a straightedge to connect the point you drew on spoke 2 to the end points on spokes 1 and 3. Continue connecting the points on the even-numbered spokes to the end points on the odd-numbered spokes on both sides.

5. Continue adding more lines to create an interesting design that has rotational symmetry.

# Assignment Sheet
## Fractions

Name_____

I began this unit on _____ (date)

Mark off each activity after you have completed it and after it has been checked.
Hand in all pages when you finish the unit.

| Lesson | Completed | Checked |
|---|---|---|
| **1.** Equivalent Fractions Review | _____ | _____ |
| **2.** Adding and Subtracting Fractions | _____ | _____ |
| **3.** Comparing Common Fractions | _____ | _____ |
| **4.** Fractions Greater Than One | _____ | _____ |
| **5.** Fractions and Fabric | _____ | _____ |
| **6.** Fraction Logic | _____ | _____ |
| **7.** Baking Cookies | _____ | _____ |
| **8.** Sharing Pizza | _____ | _____ |
| **9.** Sewing Class | _____ | _____ |
| **10.** Building a Cupboard | _____ | _____ |
| **11.** Sale Prices | _____ | _____ |
| **12.** Bargain Hunting | _____ | _____ |
| **13.** Fraction Practice | _____ | _____ |
| **14.** Fraction Fair | _____ | _____ |

I completed this unit on _____ (date)

# Equivalent Fraction Review

Name _____

**1.** Study the first example and then complete the fractions to make fractions equivalent to $\frac{1}{3}$.

    **a.** $\frac{1}{3} = \frac{4}{12}$       **b.** $\frac{1}{3} = \frac{\phantom{x}}{15}$       **c.** $\frac{1}{3} = \frac{6}{\phantom{x}}$       **d.** $\frac{1}{3} = \frac{\phantom{x}}{27}$

**2.** Study the first example and then write equivalent fractions.

    **a.** $\frac{6}{8} = \frac{3}{4}$       **b.** $\frac{16}{20} = \frac{8}{\phantom{x}}$       **c.** $\frac{6}{9} = \frac{2}{\phantom{x}}$       **d.** $\frac{5}{30} = \frac{1}{\phantom{x}}$

**3.** A fraction is in lowest terms when there is no number other than 1 that can be divided evenly into both the numerator and denominator. Write these fractions in lowest terms.

    **a.** $\frac{16}{20} = \frac{4}{5}$       **b.** $\frac{12}{18} = $____       **c.** $\frac{18}{24} = $_____       **d.** $\frac{15}{45} = $_____

Circle all the fractions in each row that are equivalent to the first fraction.

**4.** $\boxed{\dfrac{2}{4}}$    $\dfrac{6}{12}$    $\dfrac{1}{3}$    $\dfrac{1}{2}$    $\dfrac{12}{24}$    $\dfrac{5}{15}$

**5.** $\boxed{\dfrac{1}{3}}$    $\dfrac{5}{15}$    $\dfrac{3}{9}$    $\dfrac{3}{12}$    $\dfrac{4}{16}$    $\dfrac{6}{18}$

**6.** $\boxed{\dfrac{1}{5}}$    $\dfrac{4}{24}$    $\dfrac{2}{10}$    $\dfrac{15}{45}$    $\dfrac{4}{16}$    $\dfrac{3}{15}$

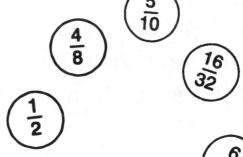

**7.** Circle all the fractions in the box that are written in lowest terms.

| | | | | |
|---|---|---|---|---|
| $\frac{10}{15}$ | $\frac{3}{4}$ | $\frac{9}{12}$ | $\frac{2}{5}$ | $\frac{6}{10}$ |
| $\frac{3}{7}$ | $\frac{3}{6}$ | $\frac{2}{3}$ | $\frac{4}{8}$ | $\frac{4}{5}$ |
| $\frac{6}{8}$ | $\frac{5}{6}$ | $\frac{8}{12}$ | $\frac{5}{8}$ | $\frac{7}{9}$ |

# Adding and Subtracting Fractions

Name_____

Zack and Katie gave two different answers to the same math problem. Here are their answers.

Zack - $\frac{1}{6} + \frac{1}{6} = \frac{2}{12}$

Katie - $\frac{1}{6} + \frac{1}{6} = \frac{2}{6}$

1. Whose answer was correct and why?_____

2. When adding or subtracting fractions with common denominators, what do you do?

   _____

   _____

3. When adding or subtracting fractions with different denominators ( like $\frac{1}{6} + \frac{1}{8}$ ), what do you need to do?

   _____

   _____

4. Write three common denominators for each pair of fractions.

   a. $\frac{3}{4}$ and $\frac{1}{8}$ _____

   b. $\frac{1}{6}$ and $\frac{5}{9}$ _____

   c. $\frac{1}{4}$ and $\frac{1}{6}$ _____

5. Use the least common denominator to add or subtract these fractions.

   a. $\frac{3}{4} + \frac{1}{8} =$ _____

   b. $\frac{1}{4} + \frac{1}{6} =$ _____

   c. $\frac{5}{9} - \frac{1}{6} =$ _____

   d. $\frac{7}{8} - \frac{2}{3}$ _____

# Comparing Common Fractions

Name_____

You can easily compare fractions if you first convert them to fractions with common denominators. So if you wanted to compare to find out which of the two fractions, $\frac{2}{3}$ or $\frac{3}{5}$, was larger, you would find a common denominator and then compare the fractions written with common denominators.

1. $\frac{2}{3} = \frac{}{15}$ and $\frac{3}{5} = \frac{}{15}$ . So $\frac{2}{3}$ is ( *greater than / less than* ) $\frac{3}{5}$ .

2. Circle the smallest fraction in each pair.

   a. $\frac{5}{6}$ or $\frac{7}{12}$      b. $\frac{3}{5}$ or $\frac{4}{7}$      c. $\frac{2}{5}$ or $\frac{4}{9}$

3. Write each group of fractions in order from smallest to largest.

   a. $\frac{1}{2}$, $\frac{1}{3}$, $\frac{2}{5}$ _____

   b. $\frac{3}{4}$, $\frac{5}{6}$, $\frac{2}{3}$ _____

   c. $\frac{3}{7}$, $\frac{1}{4}$, $\frac{5}{14}$ _____

4. You can choose one piece from a pizza cut into 5 pieces or two pieces from a pizza cut into eight pieces.

   What would you choose? Why? _____

5. You are buying a new pair of shoes. One store advertises $\frac{1}{3}$ off and the other advertises $\frac{3}{8}$ off.

   Which is the best deal? Why? _____

6. Two pies are in the refrigerator. The cherry pie has $\frac{4}{5}$ left. The blueberry has $\frac{6}{8}$ left.

   Is there more cherry or blueberry pie? _____

# Fractions Greater than One

Name _____

Fractions greater than one have a numerator that is larger than the denominator. They are fractions like $\frac{5}{3}$ . When these numbers are written as fractions, they are improper fractions. They can be changed from improper fractions to a mixed numbers by finding how many whole "1's " there are in the number.

$$\frac{5}{3} = \frac{3}{3} + \frac{2}{3} = 1\frac{2}{3} \qquad\qquad \frac{13}{4} = \frac{4}{4} + \frac{4}{4} + \frac{4}{4} + \frac{1}{4} = 3\frac{1}{4}$$

1. Change these improper fractions to mixed numbers reduced to lowest terms.

   a. $\frac{20}{8} =$ _____   b. $\frac{9}{4} =$ _____   c. $\frac{32}{6} =$ _____

   d. $\frac{22}{7} =$ _____   e. $\frac{64}{10} =$ _____   f. $\frac{57}{9} =$ _____

You can reverse this process to change a mixed number into an improper fraction.

$$2\frac{3}{4} = \frac{4}{4} + \frac{4}{4} + \frac{3}{4}. \text{ Therefore, } 2\frac{3}{4} = \frac{11}{4}.$$

2. Change these mixed numbers to improper fractions.

   a. $4\frac{2}{7} =$ _____   b. $2\frac{2}{5} =$ _____   c. $3\frac{3}{5} =$ _____

   d. $8\frac{4}{9} =$ _____   e. $8\frac{2}{3} =$ _____   f. $6\frac{4}{5} =$ _____

3. One bread recipe calls for $3\frac{1}{2}$ cups of flour and another recipe calls for $\frac{7}{3}$ cups.

   Which recipe requires the most flour? _____

# Fractions and Fabric

Name_____

If you were ordering fabric, you would not ask for $\frac{18}{4}$ yards. You would change the improper fraction $\frac{18}{4}$ to a mixed number in lowest terms and ask for $4\frac{1}{2}$ yards.

Find out how much fabric is needed in each of the following problems. Write your answers in the simplest form.

1. The 23 students in Mr. Young's class are going to make hand puppets. He will need to buy enough cloth to give each student $\frac{1}{4}$ yard.

   How many yards of cloth will he need to buy? _____ yards

2. Mr. Borzym is buying canvas to make covers for his boats. He needs $3\frac{3}{4}$ yards for the canoe cover and $9\frac{3}{4}$ yards for a cover for his fishing boat.

   How many yards of canvas will he need to buy? _____ yards

3. Mrs. Redmann is going to make matching dresses for herself and her two daughters. She needs $2\frac{1}{4}$ yards of material for her dress and $1\frac{3}{4}$ yards for each of her daughters' dresses.

   How many yards of fabric will she need to buy? _____ yards

4. Mrs. Troy is making matching bedspreads and curtains for her son's bedroom. She needs $5\frac{1}{2}$ yards for the bedspread, $4\frac{1}{2}$ yards for one window and $3\frac{1}{2}$ yards for the other window.

   How many yards of fabric will she need to buy? _____ yards

# Fraction Logic

1. The denominator is four times the numerator.
   The sum of the digits in the denominator equals the numerator.
   The sum of the numerator and denominator is less than 20.
   When reduced to lowest terms, the fraction equals $\frac{1}{4}$.

   The fraction is _____

2. Both the numerator and the denominator are multiples of 5.
   The numerator is evenly divisible by 3.
   The digit 2 appears once in the fraction.
   The fraction is equivalent to $\frac{1}{2}$

   The sum of the numerator and denominator is less than 200.

   The fraction is _____

3. The fraction is more than $\frac{1}{2}$ and less than $\frac{3}{4}$.
   It is in lowest terms.
   The numerator is one less than the denominator.

   The fraction is _____

4. The fraction is more than $\frac{1}{3}$ and less than $\frac{7}{8}$.
   The fraction is in lowest terms.
   The denominator is one more than the numerator.
   Neither the numerator or the denominator is a 3.
   The sum of the numerator and denominator is greater than 3 and less than 10.

   The fraction is _____

5. The fraction is greater than the sum of $\frac{1}{5}$ and $\frac{1}{4}$ but less than the sum of $\frac{1}{3}$ and $\frac{1}{4}$
   The numerator is one less than the denominator.
   The fraction is in lowest terms.

   The fraction is _____

Name _____

---

### Chocolate Cookies

| | |
|---|---|
| 6 oz. chocolate chips | 1 tablespoon milk |
| $\frac{3}{4}$ cup sugar | $\frac{1}{2}$ cup flour |
| 3 tablespoons butter | $\frac{1}{4}$ teaspoon salt |
| $1\frac{1}{2}$ teaspoon vanilla | $\frac{1}{4}$ teaspoon baking powder |
| 2 eggs | $\frac{1}{2}$ cup chopped nuts |

*Makes 10 cookies*

---

Rose needs to bake 20 cookies. Susie needs to bake 40 cookies. Jim needs 25 cookies, so he needs $2\frac{1}{2}$ times of each ingredient. How much of each ingredient will each person need?

| | Rose | Susie | Jim |
|---|---|---|---|
| chocolate chips | _____ | _____ | _____ |
| sugar | _____ | _____ | _____ |
| butter | _____ | _____ | _____ |
| vanilla | _____ | _____ | _____ |
| eggs | _____ | _____ | _____ |
| milk | _____ | _____ | _____ |
| flour | _____ | _____ | _____ |
| salt | _____ | _____ | _____ |
| baking powder | _____ | _____ | _____ |
| walnuts | _____ | _____ | _____ |

# Sharing Pizza

Name_____

Tony and his 3 friends ordered 3 pizzas. Each pizza was cut in 8 equal parts. What fractional part of the total pizza did each boy eat? (Reduce your answer to lowest terms.)

**Sausage**

**Mushroom**

**Pepperoni**

| | Sausage | Mushroom | Pepperoni | Fractional Part of Total Pizza |
|---|---|---|---|---|
| Tony | 2 pieces | 3 pieces | 1 piece | |
| Rick | 1 piece | 2 pieces | 1 pieces | |
| Kevin | 3 pieces | 1 piece | 4 pieces | |
| Patrick | 1 piece | 2 pieces | 2 pieces | |

1. What fractional part of the total pizza ordered was left over? _____

2. Rosa's mother ordered 3 pizzas for her slumber party. Each pizza was cut into 12 equal parts. (Reduce your answer to lowest terms.)

   a. Rosa, Carly, and Jan each ate $\frac{1}{4}$ of the total pieces of pizza. How many slices did each of them eat?_____

   b. Maria ate 6 slices of pizza. What fractional part of the pizza did she eat? _____

   c. What fractional part of the total pizza ordered was left over?_____

   d. What fractional part of **one** pizza would that be? _____

Name _____

Mrs. Hanson's advanced sewing class is working on their sewing projects. The students need to purchase various supplies.

1. Jennifer is going to make a quilt. She needs $1\frac{3}{4}$ yards of blue cotton, $2\frac{3}{8}$ yards of red cotton, $\frac{7}{8}$ yards of green cotton and $1\frac{1}{2}$ yards of white cotton.

   How much material does she need for the quilt? _____

2. Brayden bought $4\frac{1}{2}$ yards of material and used only $2\frac{3}{8}$ yards.

   How much did he have left? _____

3. Lauren bought $\frac{1}{2}$ yard of lace trim and $\frac{3}{4}$ yard of beaded trim. If all trim cost $2.00 per yard, How much did she spend? _____

4. It takes $1\frac{1}{3}$ yard of cotton to make a pair of shorts. Susan wants to make four pairs of shorts.

   How much material does she need to buy? _____

5. Larry needs $2\frac{1}{2}$ yards of denim for a pair of pants and $1\frac{1}{4}$ yards of denim for a shirt. Denim is $4.00 per yard.

   How much change would he get from a twenty-dollar bill? _____

6. Kathy bought 10 yards of material to make curtains and pillows for her room. She used $6\frac{1}{4}$ yards on the curtains.

   How much material did she have left? _____

7. A pillow can be made with $\frac{1}{2}$ yard of material.

   How many pillows can she make from the leftover material? _____

   How much material will she have left over? _____

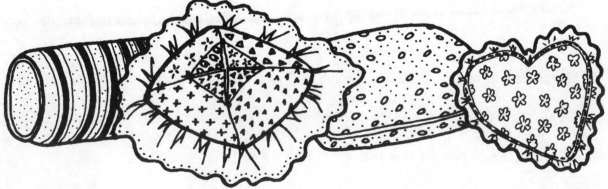

# Building a Cupboard

Name _____

Scottie's father is a carpenter. Scottie is going to help him build a cupboard. In the plans they have drawn, the front of the cupboard looks like this.

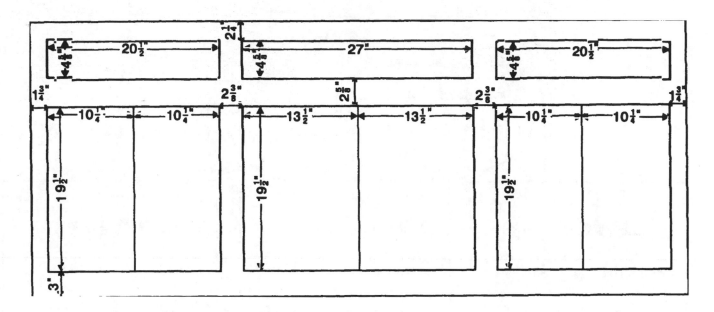

1. If they cut the three drawer fronts from one long, thin piece of wood, how long a piece of wood will they need? _____

2. If they have 2 pieces of wood that are each 35 inches long and 20 inches wide, can they cut all the cupboard doors from those two pieces? _____

3. How high will the cupboard be? _____

4. How long will the cupboard be? _____

5. The cupboard is to go on a wall that is 80 inches long. How much longer would the cupboard need to be to reach from one end of the wall to the other? _____

6. If they added $1\frac{3}{8}$ inches to each end of the cupboard, how long would the cupboard be? _____

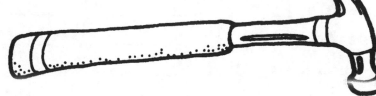

Name _____

Finding the sale price is easy if you first figure what the discount is and then subtract that from the regular price to find the sale price.

## Jeans Sale

**Regular Price**

$24.00

**Sale Price - $\frac{1}{3}$ off**

$\frac{1}{3}$ of 24.00 is $8.00.

24.00 - 8.00 = $16.00

### Shirts $\frac{1}{4}$ off

| | |
|---|---|
| silk shirt | $38.00 |
| flannel shirt | $14.80 |
| cotton T-shirt | $39.96 |

### Pants $\frac{1}{3}$ off

| | |
|---|---|
| cotton shorts | $12.99 |
| cotton pants | $15.00 |
| jeans | $24.69 |

### SHOES $\frac{1}{2}$ off

| | |
|---|---|
| sandals | $18.98 |
| tennis shoes | $49.00 |
| loafers | $35.88 |

**Use the information in the ads to find out how much you would save on each item. Then find each sale price.**

| Item Purchased | Amount Saved | Sale Price |
|---|---|---|
| silk shirt | _____ | _____ |
| flannel shirt | _____ | _____ |
| cotton T-shirt | _____ | _____ |
| cotton shorts | _____ | _____ |
| cotton pants | _____ | _____ |
| jeans | _____ | _____ |
| sandals | _____ | _____ |
| tennis shoes | _____ | _____ |
| loafers | _____ | _____ |

Name _____

You have a choice of shopping at two stores, **Don's Discount** and **Gilbert's Department Store**, which is having a sale that is supposed to be better than Don's usual discount prices. You have made a chart that shows the prices at each store and what discount Gilbert's is offering.

For each item find the sale price, determine at which store you should buy each product, and decide how much you will save by shopping at that store.

| Item | Don's Price | Gilbert's Sale Price | Gilbert's Actual Price | Store with the Best Buy | Amount Saved |
|------|-------------|----------------------|------------------------|-------------------------|--------------|
| stove | $360 | 1/3 off $525 | | | |
| toaster | $17 | 1/4 off $28 | | | |
| coffee maker | $40 | 1/4 off $52 | | | |
| refrigerator | $375 | 1/2 off $640 | | | |
| can opener | $24 | 1/3 off $31.50 | | | |
| microwave | $150 | 1/4 off $208 | | | |
| dishwasher | $250 | 1/3 off $384.99 | | | |

1. If you did all your shopping at Don's how much would you spend? _____

2. If you did all your shopping at Gilbert's, how much would you spend? _____

3. If you wanted to buy all your appliances at one store, which one would be cheaper? _____

4. How much would you save by going to the cheaper store rather than to the other store? _____

5. How much would you spend to buy all the items if you shopped at both stores, buying only the items that were the best buys at each store? _____

Name _____

1. Three friends are going together to buy a present for their teacher. They are not contributing equal amounts. Tia contributes $\frac{1}{3}$ of the total amount, Josh contributes $\frac{1}{2}$ and Carter contributes $4.00. How much did each person contribute and how much do they have to spend on a gift?

   Tia _____    Josh _____    They have _____ to spend.

2. Tommy is in a bicycle race. After one hour of racing, he realizes that $\frac{1}{2}$ of the racers are in front of him and 17 racers are in back of him.

   How many bikers are in the race? _____

3. Evie finds the exact same pair of shoes in two different stores. Store A's price is $\frac{1}{3}$ off the regular price of $69. Store B is offering the shoes for $\frac{1}{2}$ off the regular price of $86.

   Where should she buy the shoes? _____

   How much will she save by shopping at this store instead of the other one? _____

4. Your mother sets the odometer on the car at zero when you start your trip to the beach. After two hours, your mother tells you that you are $\frac{1}{3}$ of the way to the beach. You look at the odometer, which says 80.

   How far is it from your home to the beach? _____

# Fraction Fair

Name _____

1. The clown selling balloons has 24 balloons — $\frac{1}{6}$ of which are red, $\frac{1}{3}$ of which are blue, and $\frac{1}{4}$ of which are green. All the rest are yellow.

   How many balloons of each color does he have?

   _____

   _____

   The yellow balloons are what fractional part of all the balloons? _____

2. George and Albert buy a bag of candy and split it so that each person gets $\frac{1}{2}$ of the the candy. George gives $\frac{1}{3}$ of his candy to his little brother Zack. Albert eats $\frac{7}{9}$ of his candy and takes the rest of it home to his sister Emily. If Zack got 3 pieces of candy, how much did all the other people get?

   George _____        Albert _____        Emily _____

3. The line for the haunted house had 100 people in it. If $\frac{2}{10}$ of the people got in during the first ten minutes and $\frac{3}{5}$ of the original group of people got in during the second ten minutes, how many of those people were still standing in line? _____

4. Tina, Jules and Austin tried throwing dimes in cups. Tina got $\frac{3}{10}$ of the dimes in the cups, Jules got $\frac{1}{5}$ of the dimes in the cups, and Austin got $\frac{1}{4}$ of the dimes in the cups.

   Altogether, what part of the total amount of dimes that they threw in the cups did the friends get into the cups? _____

   If they started with $2.00 altogether, how much money landed in the cups? _____

   How much landed outside the cups? _____

# Assignment Sheet
## Graphing

Name _____

I began this unit on _____ (date)

Mark off each activity after you have completed it and after it has been checked. Hand in all pages when you finish the unit.

| Lesson | Completed | Checked |
|---|---|---|
| **1.** Using Symbols | _____ | _____ |
| **2.** Double Bar Graphs | _____ | _____ |
| **3.** Making a Double Bar Graph | _____ | _____ |
| **4.** Interpreting Double Line Graphs | _____ | _____ |
| **5.** Recording Data on a Double Line Graph | _____ | _____ |
| **6.** Making a Multiple Line Graph | _____ | _____ |
| **7.** Showing Parts of a Whole | _____ | _____ |
| **8.** Circle Graphs | _____ | _____ |
| **9.** Voting for Class President | _____ | _____ |
| **10.** Favorite Sports | _____ | _____ |
| **11.** Analyzing Graphs | _____ | _____ |
| **12.** Creating an Original Graph | _____ | _____ |

I completed this unit on _____ (date)

# Using Symbols

Name_____

The fifth graders in Miss Kim's class surveyed all the students in their school to find out what colors were the most popular. Students were given six colors and asked to pick their favorite. Their choices were the following.

| grade | blue | green | red | yellow | purple | pink |
|-------|------|-------|-----|--------|--------|------|
| kindergarten | 20 | 12 | 18 | 16 | 7 | 9 |
| first | 19 | 10 | 17 | 14 | 17 | 7 |
| second | 25 | 9 | 21 | 12 | 10 | 5 |
| third | 28 | 15 | 14 | 9 | 12 | 4 |
| fourth | 31 | 11 | 12 | 11 | 16 | 3 |
| fifth | 27 | 9 | 16 | 6 | 20 | 3 |

They decided to add up all the choices and make a graph that would show how many students in the whole school chose each color. There were too many students to make a symbol on the graph for each person, so they decided they would round the totals to the nearest 10 and use one symbol to represent 10 children on their graph.

Find the totals for each color, round to the nearest 10, and complete the graph below.

## Favorite Color Graph        = 10 students

| blue |
|------|
| green |
| red |
| yellow |
| purple |
| pink |

# Double Bar Graphs

Name _____

Bar graphs are often used to compare two or more things. The double bar graph below shows the enrollment of four of the elementary schools in a fast-growing city in 1985 and today. It also shows the current enrollment of Kennedy Elementary, which was built in 1990.

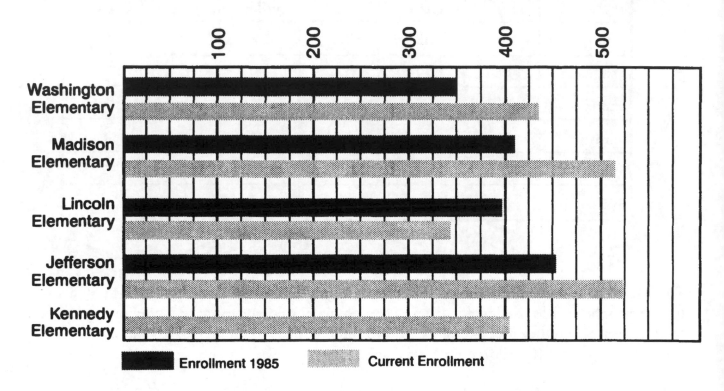

**Enrollment in Greenville Elementary Schools**

■ Enrollment 1985    ▨ Current Enrollment

1. Which is the only school where enrollment has dropped? _____

2. Which school has had the greatest increase in enrollment? _____

3. Which school has had the smallest increase in enrollment? _____

4. About how many more students are enrolled in each of these schools today than in 1985?
   Washington _____        Jefferson _____

5. About how many more students are currently enrolled in Jefferson Elementary than in Lincoln? _____

6. Which schools have enrollments of less than 450 students? _____

# Making a Double Bar Graph

Name_____

Mrs. Pumo's fifth graders decided to do a survey comparing the tastes of kindergarten and fifth grade students. They gave 50 kindergartners and 50 fifth graders six choices and asked them to choose their favorite cereals. The results are shown below.

## Kindergarten

| | | |
|---|---|---|
| Fruit Loops - 20 | Cheerios - 5 | Lucky Charms - 10 |
| Captain Crunch - 12 | Wheaties - 0 | Corn Flakes - 3 |

## Fifth Grade

| | | |
|---|---|---|
| Fruit Loops - 4 | Cheerios - 18 | Lucky Charms - 0 |
| Captain Crunch - 10 | Wheaties - 12 | Corn Flakes - 6 |

Make a double bar graph on the grid below to show the results of the survey. Be sure to include a key to show which bar represents the kindergarten and which represents fifth grade.

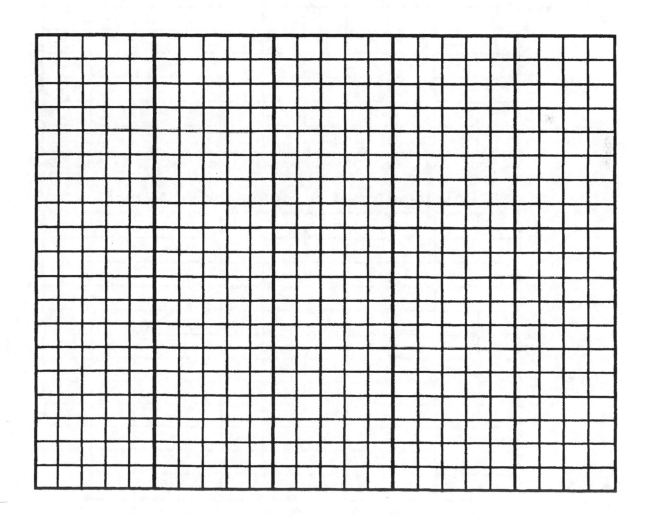

# Interpreting Double Line Graphs

Name _____

The line graphs below show the average low and high temperatures for each month of the year in two different locations in the U.S.

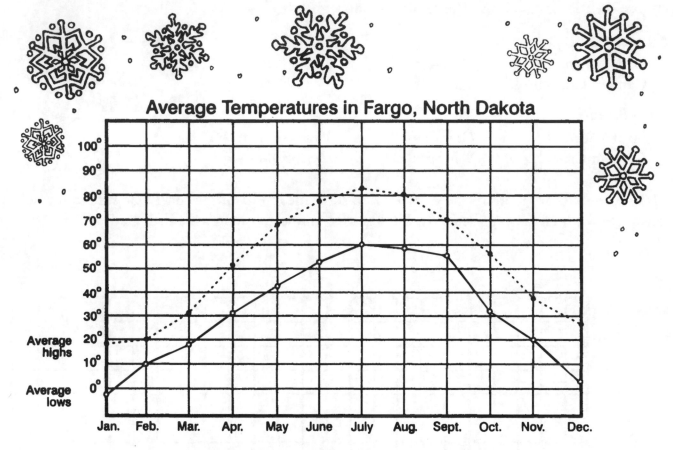

**Average Temperatures in Fargo, North Dakota**

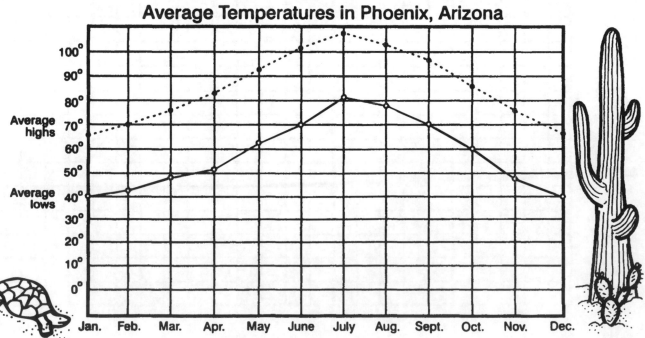

**Average Temperatures in Phoenix, Arizona**

# Interpreting Double Line Graphs
## Continued

Name_____

Use the graphs on page 52 to compare the average high and low temperatures for Fargo and Phoenix.

Compare the average **high** temperature for the two cities. Approximately how many degrees higher is the average high in Phoenix than in Fargo for each month?

### Difference in Average Highs

January          _____

June             _____

August           _____

September        _____

Compare the average **low** temperature for the two cities. Approximately how many degrees lower is the average low in Fargo than in Phoenix for each month?

### Difference in Average Lows

January          _____

March            _____

October          _____

December         _____

# Recording Data on a Double Line Graph

Name _____

Compare temperatures by gathering the data and creating a double line graph on the grid below. Choose one of the following graphing projects. Be sure to clearly label your graph so it is easy for anyone to read.

- ◆ Using a local newspaper, record the high temperature and the low temperature each day for two weeks. Use two differently colored lines to show the high and low temperatures on your graph.

- ◆ Measure the temperature at two different times of the day for two weeks. Use two differently colored lines to show the temperatures on your graph.

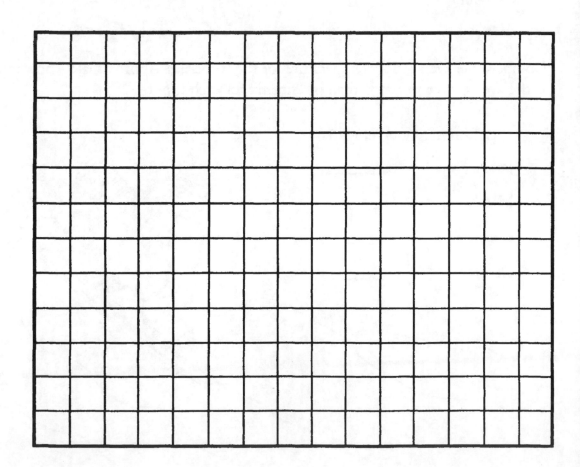

# Making a Multiple Line Graph

Name_____

The figures below show the record highs and record lows for each month of the year and the average highs and lows for each month of the year for St. Louis, Missouri.

## Record Highs

| Jan. | Feb. | Mar. | Apr. | May | June | July | Aug. | Sept. | Oct. | Nov. | Dec. |
|------|------|------|------|-----|------|------|------|-------|------|------|------|
| 78° | 82° | 89° | 92° | 98° | 105° | 115° | 108° | 103° | 93° | 86° | 75° |

## Record Lows

| Jan. | Feb. | Mar. | Apr. | May | June | July | Aug. | Sept. | Oct. | Nov. | Dec. |
|------|------|------|------|-----|------|------|------|-------|------|------|------|
| -22° | -10° | -5° | 21° | 30° | 42° | 50° | 48° | 36° | 22° | 1° | -18° |

## Average Highs

| Jan. | Feb. | Mar. | Apr. | May | June | July | Aug. | Sept. | Oct. | Nov. | Dec. |
|------|------|------|------|-----|------|------|------|-------|------|------|------|
| 39° | 42° | 54° | 67° | 75° | 85° | 89° | 88° | 80° | 70° | 54° | 41° |

## Average Lows

| Jan. | Feb. | Mar. | Apr. | May | June | July | Aug. | Sept. | Oct. | Nov. | Dec. |
|------|------|------|------|-----|------|------|------|-------|------|------|------|
| 20° | 25° | 34° | 45° | 55° | 64° | 69° | 68° | 59° | 48° | 36° | 25° |

Use a different colored line to graph each set of temperatures. Label what each line stands for.

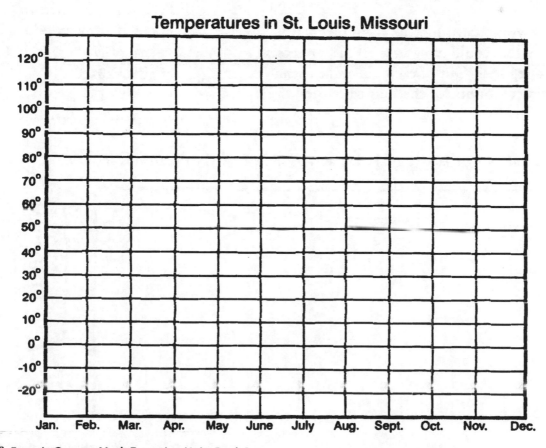

Temperatures in St. Louis, Missouri

# Showing Parts of a Whole

Name _____

The newspaper printed an article about taxes and accompanied it with a graph showing what part of each tax dollar was spent for different services.

| Public Schools 60¢ | Park District 10¢ | County Services 10¢ | City Services 15¢ | Community College 5¢ |

To construct this type of graph, you would need to find what fractional part of the whole each section represents by writing number of cents as a fractional part of a dollar. Since one dollars is 100 cents, you would show the fractions in this way.

1.  a. $60¢ = \dfrac{60}{100} = \dfrac{6}{10}$  
    b. $10¢ = \dfrac{10}{100} = \underline{\hspace{1cm}}$

    c. $15¢ = \underline{\hspace{1cm}} = \dfrac{3}{20}$  
    d. $5¢ = \underline{\hspace{1cm}} = \underline{\hspace{1cm}}$

2. Is the total amount spent on the park district, county services, city services, and community college more or less than what is spent on public schools? _____

When Curt wrote down how he spent his money, he found that he could categorize all his purchases into four categories. Out of each dollar, he spent the following amounts for the four categories.

- ◆ entertainment - 40¢
- ◆ snacks - 25¢
- ◆ gifts - 20¢
- ◆ other - 15¢

3. Use the following space to make a graph to show how Curt spent his money.

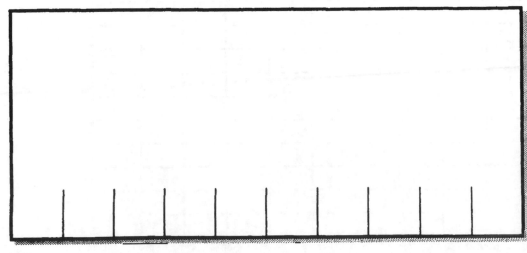

56

# Circle Graphs

Name_____

Circle graphs are often used to show fractional parts of a whole. The number of degrees in the central angles of each part of the graph always add up to 360º.

To make a circle graph, you need to find out what fractional part of the whole each section represents. Then you need to find out how to express that fraction as part of 360º.

1. If you wanted to make a graph of a dollar broken into sections to show group A spends 25¢, group B spends 10¢, group C spends 50¢, and groups D, E, and F spend 5¢ each, you would do the following calculations.

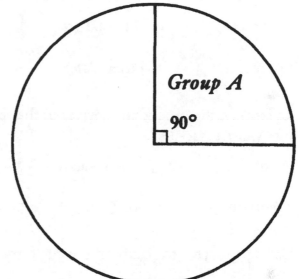

$25¢ = \dfrac{25}{100} = \dfrac{1}{4}$ and $\dfrac{1}{4}$ of 360º = 90º

$50¢ = \dfrac{50}{100} = \dfrac{1}{2}$ and $\dfrac{1}{2}$ of 360º = _____

$10¢ = \dfrac{10}{100} = \dfrac{1}{10}$ and $\dfrac{1}{10}$ of 360º = _____

$5¢ = \dfrac{5}{100} =$ ____ and ____ of 360º = _____

2. Draw in the missing sections on the graph.

3. A group of 48 students was asked what type of movie they liked best. Comedies were chosen by 24 people. Science fictions was chosen by 16, and westerns were the favorite of 8 people.

   a. Find the fractional part of the whole that liked each movie.
   b. Determine how many degrees each section should be.
   c. Draw and label the graph.
   d. Give the graph a title.

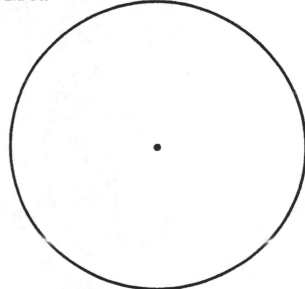

# Voting for Class President

Name _____

Four students were candidates in the election for class president. The results of the election were

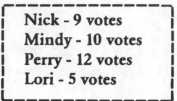

Nick - 9 votes
Mindy - 10 votes
Perry - 12 votes
Lori - 5 votes

To show the election results on a circle graph, we need to know the following.

1. Determine the total number to be shown in the graph. Total number of people voting = _____

2. Determine what fractional part of the total vote each candidate got.

   9 votes is $\frac{9}{36}$ or $\frac{1}{4}$ of the total votes          10 votes is _____ of the total votes

   12 votes is _____ the total votes          5 votes is _____ the total votes

3. Determine the number of degrees of the circle graph to be represented by each candidate. Every circle has 360°.

   9 votes is $\frac{1}{4}$ of 360°, which equals 90°          10 votes is _____ of 360°, or _____°

   5 votes is _____ of 360°, or _____°          12 votes is _____ of 360°, or _____°

4. Use a protractor to complete the circle graph.

*Nick*

90°

# Favorite Sports

Name_____

The gym teachers at Hillside School surveyed the 6th graders to find out what was their favorite sport to play. The results are shown in the chart.

1. Find the fractional part of the whole group that chose each sport.

2. Find how many degrees out of a circle each fraction would equal.

3. Use a protractor to show the results in a circle graph.

| Sport | Number of Votes | Fraction of Total | Number of Degrees |
|-------|-----------------|-------------------|-------------------|
| baseball | 30 | | |
| football | 25 | | |
| basketball | 45 | | |
| soccer | 15 | | |
| others | 5 | | |

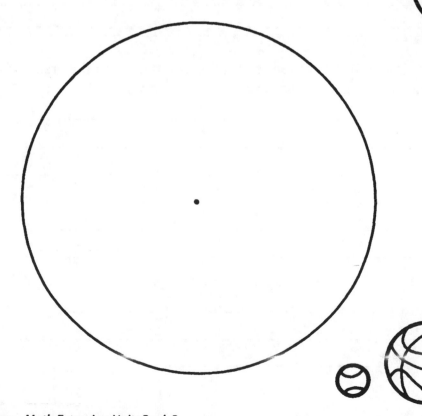

# Analyzing Graphs

Name _____

Find a graph in a newspaper or magazine.
Cut it out and glue it on this page.

On the lines below, write five questions about the data shown on the graph. Have another student answer the questions, and then you check the answers.

1. _____

_____

2. _____

_____

3. _____

_____

4. _____

_____

5 . _____

_____

# Creating an Original Graph

Name_____

To make an original graph, you would do the following:

## GATHER DATA

You could get data from a newspaper, atlas, almanac, or encyclopedia. For example:

- ◆ points scored by favorite basketball players
- ◆ distances from a major city to other cities
- ◆ populations of cities, comparing growth from one time to another

You could gather your own data by surveying people about a given topic. For example:

- ◆ favorite color, cereal, TV show, singing group
- ◆ types of pets owned
- ◆ place they would most like to visit

HINT: *When you do a survey, it is best to limit the number of choices.*

## DETERMINE THE TYPE OF GRAPH

After you have the data, you must decide on which type of graph to use to best show the information. For example:

- ◆ Line graphs work well for showing changes in information (such as daily temperatures).

- ◆ Circle graphs work well for showing parts of a whole (such as what parts of a day are spent in various activities).

- ◆ Bar graphs and picture graphs work well for comparing things.

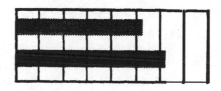

## MAKE THE GRAPH

---

### PROJECT

**Collect data to create an original graph.
Decide what type of graph you think would be the best
to make to show the information. Make your graph on
another sheet of paper or on graph paper.**

---

# Answers

## Feeding the Animals - pg. 7
1. 26,000 pounds     $8,125
2. $144,000     $12,000
3. 10 pounds     $5,000
4. 27,000 pounds

## Planning a Trip - pg. 8
1. $532
2. No - needs $26.00

## Patriotic Puzzles - pg. 9
1. 36 columns     2. 555 feet
3. 3,175 seats     4. 90 years
5. 24 routes

## Planning a Picnic - pg. 10
| | | |
|---|---|---|
| plates | 9 pkg. | 8 extra |
| napkins | 7 pkg. | 12 extra |
| cups | 3 pkg. | 8 extra |
| forks | 5 pkg. | 20 extra |
| hot dogs | 13 | |
| buns | 13 | |
| soda | 4 cases and 1 carton | |
| chips | 8 | |
| cookies | 9 | |
| ice cream | 9 | |

## Summer Job - pg. 11
1. $210     2. $96.70
3. $182.20 savings     $91.10 checking
4. $2,170
5. Brother earns $198 per week or $1,980 for 10 weeks, which is more than Jenny will take home once taxes are taken out.

## Field Trip - pg. 12
1. 14 parents     4. $287
2. 130     5. 11 tables
3. $273     6. $644
    2 extra seats     7. no

## All Aboard - pg. 13
1. 24 trains     3. 228 miles
2. 1 is under 6 years     4. 14 adults, 4 children

## Class Store - pg. 14
1. $90     5. $36.00
2. $35.52     6. $27.50
3. $17.46     7. $239.33
4. $32.85     8. $160.67

## Basketball Game - pg. 15
| | |
|---|---|
| Henley - 11 | Hunt - 8 |
| Rodriguez - 12 | Williams - 10 |
| Cassidy - 22 | Delaney - 20 |
| Johnson - 12 | Gonzales - 19 |
| Yung - 18 | Kaminski - 13 |
| Wildcat total - 75 | Huskie total - 70 |

## Basketball Game, continued
1. Wildcats - 13     Huskies - 12
2. Cassidy, Delaney
3. Wildcat - 15     Huskies - 14

## Buying Tile - pg. 16
| | | |
|---|---|---|
| kitchen | 192 sq. ft. | $528.00 |
| child's bath | 48 sq. ft. | $108.00 |
| parent's bath | 80 sq. ft. | $200.00 |

1. $836.00
2. $20.00
3. Answers will vary.     4. Answers will vary.

## Buying Carpet - pg. 17
| | | | |
|---|---|---|---|
| family | 288 sq. ft. | 32 sq. yd. | $800 |
| dining | 144 sq. ft | 16 sq. yd. | $400 |
| parents | 252 sq. ft. | 28 sq. yd. | $616 |
| Leah | 126 sq. ft. | 14 sq. yd. | $224 |
| John | 108 sq. ft. | 12 sq. yd. | $192 |

1. $2,232

## Redecorating - pg. 18
1. 512 sq. ft.
2. 3 gallons
3. 252 sq. ft.     28 sq. yd.
4. 64 ft.

| | | |
|---|---|---|
| paint | 3 | $26.97 |
| carpet | 28 | $530.60 |
| border | 5 | $39.75 |

## Drawing Angles - pg. 21
1. ∠XYZ = 42°     3. ∠JKL = 168°
2. ∠TQR = 90°     4. ∠FDG = 133°

## Drawing Pairs of Angles - pg. 22

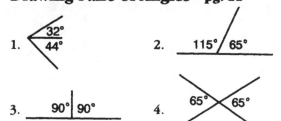

## Types of Triangles - pg. 23

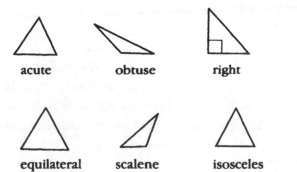

acute     obtuse     right

equilateral     scalene     isosceles

## Naming Triangles - pg. 24
1. acute isosceles, acute equilateral, acute scalene
   obtuse isosceles, obtuse equilateral, obtuse scalene
   right isosceles, right equilateral, right, scalene
2. obtuse equilateral and right equilateral
3. Answers will vary.

## Triangle Experiment - pg. 25
1. all
2. 180°
3. a. 28°      b. 90°      c. 13°
4. 60°
5. No - The sum of two of the angles would be greater
   than 180°, which is the sum of all three angles of a
   triangle.

## Missing Angles - pg. 26
1. x = 160°
2. y = 138°
3. a = 155°      b = 25°      c = 155°
4. w = 60°
5. x = 68°
6. x = 61°      y = 29°      z = 90°
7. a = 53°      b = 37°
8. x = 58°      y = 40°      z = 82°

## Regular Polygons and Angles - pg. 27
pentagon    5        72°     108°    540°
hexagon     6        60°     120°    720°
octagon              8       45°     135°    1080°
decagon     10       36°     144°    1440°

## Lines of Symmetry - pg. 28
1.       2. 3

3. square - 4 lines      pentagon - 5 lines
   hexagon - 6 lines     octagon - 8 lines

## Symmetry Experiment - pg. 29
1. yes                4. a, b, d, f
2. no                 5. yes
3. 3

## Rotational Symmetry and Design - pg. 30
1. position 2         4. yes
2. 8 total            5. 4
3. no

## Hexagon / Decagon Design - pgs. 31-32

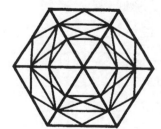
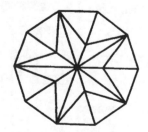

## Equivalent Fraction Review - pg. 34
1. b. $\frac{5}{15}$      c. $\frac{6}{18}$      d. $\frac{9}{27}$

2. b. $\frac{8}{10}$      c. $\frac{2}{3}$      d. $\frac{1}{6}$

3. b. $\frac{2}{3}$      c. $\frac{3}{4}$      d. $\frac{1}{3}$

4. $\frac{6}{12}$, $\frac{1}{2}$, $\frac{12}{24}$

5. $\frac{5}{15}$, $\frac{3}{9}$, $\frac{6}{18}$

6. $\frac{2}{10}$, $\frac{3}{15}$

7. $\frac{3}{4}$      $\frac{2}{5}$      $\frac{3}{7}$      $\frac{2}{3}$

   $\frac{4}{5}$      $\frac{5}{6}$      $\frac{7}{9}$      $\frac{5}{8}$

## Adding and Subtracting Fractions - pg. 35
1. Katie; Zack added numerators and denominators
2. Add or subtract the numerators.
3. Find a common denominator and then add or subtract the numerators.
4. a.  8, 16, 24, 32 . . .
   b. 18, 36, 54, 72 . . .
   c. 12, 24, 36, 48 . . .
5. a. $\frac{7}{8}$           b. $\frac{5}{12}$

   c. $\frac{7}{18}$          d. $\frac{5}{24}$

## Comparing Common Fractions - pg. 36
1. $\frac{2}{3} = \frac{10}{15}$      $\frac{3}{5} = \frac{9}{15}$      greater

2. a. $\frac{7}{12}$      b. $\frac{4}{7}$      c. $\frac{2}{5}$

3. a. $\frac{1}{3}$, $\frac{2}{5}$, $\frac{1}{2}$

   b. $\frac{2}{3}$, $\frac{3}{4}$, $\frac{5}{6}$

   c. $\frac{1}{4}$, $\frac{5}{14}$, $\frac{3}{7}$

4. 2 pieces cut in eighths

5. $\frac{3}{8}$

6. cherry pie

## Fractions Greater Than one - pg. 37
1. a. $2\frac{1}{2}$      b. $2\frac{1}{4}$      c. $5\frac{1}{3}$

   d. $3\frac{1}{7}$      e. $6\frac{2}{5}$      f. $6\frac{1}{3}$

2. a. $\frac{30}{7}$      b. $\frac{12}{5}$      c. $\frac{18}{5}$

   d. $\frac{76}{9}$      e. $\frac{26}{3}$      f. $\frac{34}{5}$

3. $3\frac{1}{2}$ cups

## Fractions and Fabric - pg. 38

1. $5\frac{3}{4}$ yds.      3. $5\frac{3}{4}$ yds.

2. $13\frac{1}{2}$ yds.     4. $13\frac{1}{2}$ yds.

## Fraction Logic - pg. 39

1. $\frac{3}{12}$     4. $\frac{4}{5}$

2. $\frac{60}{120}$     5. $\frac{1}{2}$

3. $\frac{2}{3}$

## Baking Cookies - pg. 40

|  | Rose | Susie | Jim |
|---|---|---|---|
| chips (oz.) | 12 | 24 | 15 |
| sugar (cups) | $1\frac{1}{2}$ | 3 | $1\frac{7}{8}$ |
| butter (tbs.) | 6 | 12 | $7\frac{1}{2}$ |
| vanilla (tsp.) | 3 | 6 | $3\frac{3}{4}$ |
| eggs | 4 | 8 | 5 |
| milk (tbs.) | 2 | 4 | $2\frac{1}{2}$ |
| flour (cups) | 1 | 2 | $1\frac{1}{4}$ |
| salt (tsp.) | $\frac{1}{2}$ | 1 | $\frac{5}{8}$ |
| bak. pow. (tsp.) | $\frac{1}{2}$ | 1 | $\frac{5}{8}$ |
| walnuts (cups) | 1 | 2 | $1\frac{1}{4}$ |

## Sharing Pizza - pg. 41

Tony - 1/4     Rick 1/6

Kevin - 1/3     Patrick - 5/24

1. 1/24 (1 piece)

2. a. 9     b. 1/6

   c. 1/12     d. 1/4 (3 pieces)

## Sewing Class - pg. 42

1. $6\frac{1}{2}$     5. $5.00

2. $2\frac{1}{8}$     6. $3\frac{3}{4}$

3. $2.50     7. 7 pillows;

4. $5\frac{1}{3}$     $\frac{1}{4}$ yd. left over

## Building a Cupboard - pg. 43

1. 68 in     4. $76\frac{1}{4}$

2. yes     5. $3\frac{3}{4}$

3. 32 in.     6. 79 in.

## Sale Prices - pg. 44

| silk shirt | $9.50 | $28.50 |
|---|---|---|
| flannel shirt | $3.70 | $11.10 |
| cotton T-shirt | $9.99 | $29.97 |
| cotton shorts | $4.33 | $8.66 |
| cotton pants | $5.00 | $10.00 |
| jeans | $8.23 | $16.46 |
| sandals | $9.49 | $9.49 |
| tennis shoes | $24.50 | $24.50 |
| loafers | $17.94 | $17.94 |

## Bargain Hunting - pg. 45

| stove | $350 | Gilbert | $10 |
|---|---|---|---|
| toaster | $21 | Don | $4 |
| coffee | $39 | Gilbert | $1 |
| refrigerator | $320 | Gilbert | $55 |
| can opener | $21 | Gilbert | $3 |
| microwave | $156 | Don | $6 |
| dishwasher | $256.66 | Don | $6.66 |

1. $1,216        4. $52.34
2. $1,163.66      5. $1,147.00
3. Gilbert's

## Fraction Practice - pg. 46

1. Tia - $8     Josh - $12     total $24
2. 36
3. Store B     $3
4. 240 miles

## Fraction Fair - pg. 47

1, 4 red        8 blue        6 green
   6 yellow     1/4 yellow
2. George - 6    Albert - 7     Emily - 2
3. 20 people
4. 3/4     $1.50     50¢

## Using Symbols - pg. 49

Graph should show the following numbers:
blue - 150 (15 crayons)     green - 66 (7 crayons)
red - 98 (10 crayons)     yellow - 68 (7 crayons)
purple - 82 (8 crayons)     pink - 31 (3 crayons)

## Double Bar Graph - pg. 50

1. Lincoln     4. Washington - 85; Jefferson - 70
2. Madison     5. about 180
3. Jefferson     6. Washington, Lincoln, Kennedy

## Making a Double - Bar Graph - pg. 51

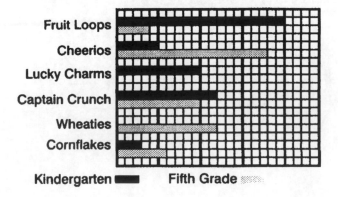

Fruit Loops  
Cheerios  
Lucky Charms  
Captain Crunch  
Wheaties  
Cornflakes  

Kindergarten ▬     Fifth Grade ▦

## Interpreting a Double Line Graph - pg. 52-53

Answers may vary by a couple of degrees.

| highs | | lows | |
|-------|------|-------|------|
| Jan. | 48° | Jan. | 43° |
| June | 23° | March | 31° |
| Aug. | 22° | Oct. | 27° |
| Sept. | 28° | Dec. | 37° |

## Recording Data/Double Line Graph - pg. 54
Answers will vary.

## Making a Multiple Line Graph - pg. 55

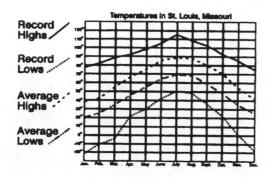

## Showing Parts of a Whole - pg. 56
1. b. 1/10        c. 15/100        d. 5/100 = 1/20
2. less
3.

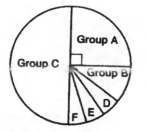

## Circle Graphs - pg. 57
1. 180°
   36°
   1/20, 1/20, 18°

2 and 3.

Group A = 90°        Group B = 36°
Group C = 180°        Groups D, E, F = 18°

Comedies = 180°
Science Fiction = 120°
Westerns = 60°

## Voting for Class President - pg. 58
1. 36
2. 10/36 = 5/18          12/36 = 1/3
   5/36 = 5/36
3. 5/18 = 100°        5/36 = 50°
   1/3 = 120°
4. Nick = 90°        Mindy = 100°
   Perry = 120°        Lori = 50°

## Favorite Sports - pg. 59

| baseball | 30 | 1/4 | 90° |
|----------|----|----|-----|
| football | 25 | 5/24 | 75° |
| basketball | 45 | 9/24 = 3/8 | 135° |
| soccer | 15 | 3/24 = 1/8 | 45° |
| other | 5 | 1/24 | 15° |

## Analyzing Graphs - pg. 60
Answers will vary.

## Creating an Original Graph - pg. 61
Answers will vary.

Printed in the United States
by Baker & Taylor Publisher Services